I0559963

Work That Body Now!
Looking And Feeling Your Best at Any Age, Shape or Size

Mary A. Whitfield

Dedicated To

My Children For Your
"Endless Love"

Table Of Contents

INTRODUCTION..1

Wake-Up Call 2

SECTION ONE 6

What Shape Is My Body? 7

You are a Curvaceous Fruit? 9

Who's That Women in the Mirror? 12

How Does My Culture Affect My Shape? 16

African American Women 19

Caucasian Women 23

Asian Women.. 25

SECTION TWO 27

What If I Don't Like My Shape? 28

SECTION THREE 35

Principles to Jump Start A New You 36

SECTION FOUR 45

How Does My Body Really Work? 46

Should My Heart Beat This Fast?............................... 48

Is Exercise on My List of New Year's Resolutions? ... 50

Does Overweight Mean I'm Obese? 52

SECTION FIVE... 56

How Do I Avoid Conking Out? 57

SECTION SIX... 62

Now That I Got One Foot Off the Ground, What's Next?...... 63

SECTION SEVEN... 66

Should I Even Wear a Bathing Suit?...67

SECTION EIGHT **69**

Standing Ovations 70

What If I Finally Find Mr. Right?...70

What If I Get Divorced? 73

What If I Want to Have a Baby? 75

What if I'm Invited to A Formal Affair?...77

How Can I Prevent Losing My Mind? 79

Conclusion..83

Abdominal Specialization Routine...85

Leg Specialization Routine 88

Park Circuit Workout...90

Resistance Band and Barbell Exercises 94

Work That Body Journal 95

References...96

Disclaimer: Consult your healthcare provider before starting any exercise program. The opinions in this book are my own and do not reflect the views of others

INTRODUCTION

Wake-Up Call

I wrote this book several years ago while I was still working as a Registered Nurse and Fitness Trainer. Along with a hectic work schedule, some plain old procrastination, and lack of motivation, it lived quietly on my flash drive. After 35 years in healthcare, Covid-19 and a renewed spark of excitement about sharing my story, I dusted off the flash drive, cranked up the laptop, came out of retirement, and now I'm back in the saddle. What's interesting is that besides updating some statistics and adding some new images, the information I'm sharing is still as relevant today as it was then. That's the beauty of living a healthy lifestyle.

Once upon a time, at one of my favorite resorts in Palm Springs, California, I was sitting by the pool reading and just relaxing while watching families, couples, and singles of all ages and nationalities enjoy the sun and the fun. Then I started to notice how the majority of them, young and old, tall and short, had something very much in common, that of being overweight and out of shape. The women had flabby arms and legs, potbellies, droopy breast, back cleavage, sagging buttocks, and cellulite in places that I don't care to mention. However, that didn't stop them from wearing bathing suits. I'm talking bikinis, thongs, and halter-tops. The men on the other hand, looked like beached whales. They had abdomens that were twice the size of a nine-month pregnancy. I even saw babies and young kids that were already on their way to living a life of obesity and the complications that come with it.

My mind started working overtime. I began to wonder if any of these women or men would have taken better physical care of themselves if they knew how they would end up looking years later. Did they know that lack of physical activity and poor eating habits would have a major impact on their future lives? Did they even care? Would it have made a difference if they knew they could possibly live longer and healthier, allowing them to spend more quality time with their families, especially their grandchildren? In the midst of this contemplation, I had my "epiphany," and I wanted to write about it. I wanted to say, "Hey, this is your wake-up call. Look around. Look at yourself. You don't have to end up like this, and if you are already there, you can do something about it. It's never too late. I decided to scare some young women straight and some older women into reality faster than they could say, "Who opened Pandora's Box?" I took pen to paper by the pool that very day.

Sometime later, I was sitting at a favorite restaurant with two friends when I first shared my desire to write this book. I briefly described how young women could get ahead of the game by starting now and older women can look and feel better than ever if they really took eating habits and exercise seriously. They laughed at me and talked about how after a certain age women don't care about how they look, especially after they get married and have a couple of babies. "You should write about childhood obesity, something that is really important. Just look around at the women in this restaurant, they are fat and they know it, and they don't care," they said. I was shocked and mortified. Was this true? Why have so many women stopped caring about their health, appearance, and how it affects their lives? This really ignited my passion to get young women to start working out now and older women to work on what they have.

Over the years, I have heard all the excuses for being out of shape and overweight. Such as "I was busy working and raising a family," "I never liked exercising," "I was born fat," "I always look

3

clumsy when I work out," "I've been married for umpteen years so I don't have to stay in shape," " I worked all day already and exercise is like work," and so on and so on and so on. Nevertheless, as we know, there's no excuse. In a perfect world, we should all want to exercise and live a long and healthy life, but as truth would have it, it becomes the last thing on our personal agendas. I understand that there are many reasons why a woman may be overweight outside of the dreaded "couch potato" syndrome. Some of these may be for medical conditions.

Popular weight loss programs, diets, and other remedies offer the false hope of dropping pounds quickly with little to no personal effort. That's probably why there are so many of them with such little success, which ultimately lead to feelings of failure and discouragement. The popular weight reduction surgeries require extreme lifestyle changes which work for some and not for others. Natural weight loss takes commitment, discipline, and physical work to lose it and then to keep it off. When I train women of all sizes, ages, and backgrounds, I create a workout routine and diet plan that is unique to their personal history, goals, and abilities. Not every woman who hire me wants to get to a size three, lose a hundred pounds to attend a class reunion or fit into a bridesmaid's dress in 60 days, but some do. The ones that want instant results end up discouraged and quitting, not to speak of the time and money they wasted. The others focus on setting and reaching realistic and attainable goals, keeping them motivated and coming back. My claim to fame is to have them to identify the area or areas of their bodies they consider their best assets. Next, they choose the areas they want to isolate and concentrate on to improve. They love this concept; it is the opposite of what they'd experienced with others trainers. These trainers worked them out so hard they could barely walk for days. The sooner women get started and stay with some type of regular exercise routine, the more they will appreciate their bodies as they get older and as their bodies start to change.

According to a National Health and Nutrition Survey, over two-thirds of adults in the United States are overweight or obese. In addition, even more shocking, 35% of these are young girls and women. Not only is being overweight unattractive, it is totally unhealthy, causing diabetes, heart disease, high cholesterol, cancer, stroke, and even death. At least 75% of African-American, Caucasian, and Hispanic women over the age of 20 are overweight. This is scary, isn't it? To add insult to injury is the psychological issues that plague many of these women because of their negative self-image.

Today there are so many ways to get in and stay in shape. You are bound to find something that you love doing from aerobics, dancing, home workouts, running and walking, gardening, virtual exercises, and so much more. Moreover, don't forget that the mind, body, and spirit works as a whole. If you empower the mind, the body will follow. There are all kinds of techniques to nurture this connection, including yoga, meditation, self-affirmations, and much more, to achieve a harmonious balance between body and soul. This is a fun book about identifying and enhancing your best assets, creating a personal and realistic workout routine that fits your body shape and lifestyle, discovering ways to lift self-esteem, improve self-image, and mostly to take charge of your health through exercise, education, and empowerment. So sit back, relax, laugh, and enjoy the journey.

SECTION ONE

What Shape Is My Body?

There is certainly one thing true about the way we look as humans, and that is we come in all shapes and sizes. I can't even begin to imagine a world where we all look exactly alike. We are wonderfully created to reflect a rich connection to a unique heritage and ancestry. My sister Joyce always says, "It's in the "501s." Not the kind you wear, the ones you're born with. You know the genes, DNA (Deoxyribonucleic Acid). Our genes, and for us women, our hormones, mostly estrogen, produce the right environment for our unique physical destiny. So rather, we like it or not, it's what we are born with. The estrogen is responsible for the development of our reproductive functions as well as the shape of our breasts and hips. Small amounts of the male hormone testosterone promote muscle development in our arms, legs, back, and other parts of our body. We need a perfect balance of all three to be the beautiful creatures we are meant to be.

In Western society, the female physique is associated with being curvaceous, lean, and toned. For most women and girls, this is not only unrealistic but also unattainable for most. I really like the 12 Realistic Body Shapes Chart by Nina Squirrelly. It really shows how diverse women shapes can be with fluctuating degrees of variations. For example, an oval shape in which the waist is larger than the breast and hips with narrow shoulders (reminds me of the Michelin Tire Man) or the diamond shape that has narrow shoulders, large waist, and large hips (the perfect snowman). You are bound to find your shape, or someone you know is one of these distinctive figures. Google it.

As we get older and our hormone levels change and ultimately diminish altogether, we inevitably see a significant impact on our shape, some good, some not so good. This is mostly caused by the redistribution and storage of the body's fat. This is so evident during and after pregnancy, when a woman's body can go through a complete transformation. Of course, after menopause, natural, chemical, or surgical, fat redistribution is common in the buttocks, hips, thighs, and, unfortunately, the waist. This is so important to know because so many women get excited about no longer having a menstrual cycle, but don't realize that they have to watch their food intake and exercise even more now than ever. Can you relate? I certainly can.

Identifying and accepting your true body shape is essential to choosing the correct clothes and swimwear. Even more so, which exercises can help build and reshape your body to accentuate your best features. It took me a while, but I learned that I could work with my shape rather than against it. With increasing age, regular exercise, and good nutrition, I've come to appreciate my body and how fabulous I look in and out of my clothes, at least to myself, which is all that matters at this point of the game.

It's so very ironic that as I was typing this and doing some research online, I came across a recent article entitled "Body Hair, Flab, and more: Store mannequins get 'real' makeovers." According to Today Style, the once one-size-fits-all mannequins were long overdue for a makeover. We can look forward to seeing everything from pubic hair, tattoos, thick waists, sagging breasts, and believe it or not back fat, also known as the dreaded "back cleavage" in the fitness world. The hope is to give shoppers a more realistic idea of what they would look like in certain clothing, including swimwear. The traditional mannequins were a perfect size 6 with a 36-26-36 bust-waist-hip measurement. Unless you are Marilyn Monroe, many women only see this figure in their dreams. The new mannequin' shapes have smaller, flatter breasts and perfect imperfections like belly pouches and other bulges. How realistic is that? Over time, the ideal body shape will become obsolete and will continue to evolve. I'm just hoping this doesn't give women permission to become too complacent with being overweight and out of shape.

You are a Curvaceous Fruit?

My cousin would always say she has the "Jones Family legs." What did she mean by that? Well, the girls in her family all had full-sized upper bodies, thighs, and calves, but very skinny ankles. She hated wearing dresses that showed this self-proclaimed flaw in her shape. The fact that most of the world, being obsessed with the perfect body shape, doesn't help those of us who don't fall into that category. The truth we are born with the shape we have. When our bodies get out of the shape, this is when we have the problem. Therefore, in a desperate attempt to correct what is genetically normal, many women desperately seek ways to manipulate and alter their bodies. Oh! Don't get me wrong; I was an operating room nurse for a cosmetic surgeon who did some amazing work. I'm just saying it should be an enhancement, not a recreation. Sometimes cosmetic and other procedures work, and sometimes they don't, leaving undesirable results. Just ask some very well known celebrities. However, identifying and accepting your body shape will help you to develop realistic goals when it comes to nutrition and exercise.

The four common body shapes for women are banana, apple, pear, and hourglass. However, body shapes can consist of a combination of shapes as well. The four basic shapes can be found in every culture and ethnic group. The bust, waist, and hips are the structural points of the female body, and the circumference of these areas defines the overall shape. Although two women may have the same basic body shape, the distribution of fat and muscle will give them a totally different appearance. As increasing proportions of fat are dispersed among the various shapes, the body experiences a metamorphosis, commonly referred to as

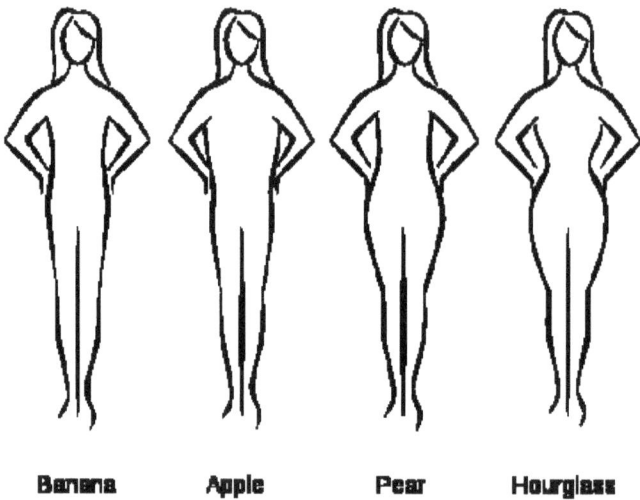

| Banana | Apple | Pear | Hourglass |

being out of shape or obese.

Photo Courtesy of Wikipedia

Appetizing Apple – V Shape (downward triangle)

This fruity shape has broad shoulders and bust with narrow hips—slim legs and thighs. Weight distribution can be seen in the face, abdomen, and chest areas. The presence of the male hormone is commonly present, possibly giving this woman a slight advantage when it comes to physical strength. Examples: Naomi Campbell, Angelina Jolie Pitt

Lean Banana- straight Line (rectangular)

With this shape, the waist tends to be smaller than the hips and boobs. The male hormone also influences this body shape with fat distribution predominately in the abdomen, face, chest, and buttocks. Example: Nicole Kidman, Cameron Diaz

Juicy Pear- A shape (triangle upward)

Have you ever heard the term "Thunder Thighs" or "Baby Got Back? Well, that describes this shape to a tee. The hips are big, and fat has a tendency to spread in the butt, hips, and thighs. Women with this shape are especially admired for their significantly large bottom and hefty thighs. Examples: Jennifer Lopez, Beyoncé.

Timeless Hourglass- X shape (opposing triangles)

This shape sports a narrow waist, accentuating the hips and boobs. Most women would die for a shape like this, including me. Fat is distributed around the upper and lower body. Example: Raquel Welch, Scarlet Johansson

Personally, I fall into the apple shape category, one that I've disliked most of my life; that is, until years later when I came to appreciate not having to struggle with being overweight. I was straight up and down, no hips or accompanying derriere and all of 118 lbs. in my late thirties. Let me not forget to mention my bony legs. My legs were so skinny; my brothers used to call me skeleton woman. In the eighties, I started working out after successfully giving up smoking with the help of one of the physicians I worked with. He was also an inventor and had developed a recipe for the first stop smoking gum, long before Nicorette. This homemade reusable gum consisted of black tar and mint with no nicotine, and to my amazement, it worked. I never picked up another cigarette again. I don't believe his invention ever made it to the big market, but as far as I'm concerned, it was a winner. Here I am 10 years later, not bad.

As medicine and technology continue to expand, there will continue to be new and exciting ways to reshape your body and totally transform the way you look and feel. However, as a nurse and personal trainer, I am a huge advocate of reshaping the body naturally through healthy eating, body sculpting, and good old fashion cardio exercises. That's not to say I won't entertain a little nip-tuck when father time catches up. However, positively transforming your body no matter what your shape can give you a great sense of power, control, and satisfaction. You can fall in love with the women in the mirror and feel so good about what you have been able to accomplish.

Who's That Women in the Mirror?

Many of the women and occasionally some of the men that I've had the pleasure to train frequently voiced dissatisfaction with their self-image. In these particular situations, it was actually positive because it motivated them to engage in healthier lifestyle behaviors, especially exercising. However, for others, the desire to have a healthy self-image without putting in the effort often leads to depression, binge eating, drinking, and what I call "Exercise Rage." Exercise Rage describes people that I have witnessed become so obsessed with losing a lot of weight instantaneously, that they engage in extreme workout routines, quickly burning themselves out. These people had not worked out in years, if ever.

So many factors can affect our weight loss or gain, everything from genetics, culture, health conditions, lifestyle choices, personal beliefs, and more. All of these directly influence how and what we believe and feel about ourselves. One myth is that how much we weigh, especially if one is obese, is under a person's total control. As you just read, that is not always true. There is nothing more detrimental to a person's self-image than the media with its fascination with the perfect body image. Studies have shown that just several minutes of television can negatively alter a girl's or woman's body perceptions. Furthermore, on television, overweight people often find themselves the butt of jokes and are often ridiculed. They are portrayed as binge eaters, fat losers, and the black sheep. I can't think of one nude love scene that involves two or even one overweight people. On the other hand, the so-called "ideal body image" is thrown into our faces twenty-four hours, seven days a week through reality television, glamour magazines, billboards, exercise infomercial, and other advertisements.

Not only do overweight women have to contend with their own struggles with an altered self-image, but others have also been known to inflict negative attitudes and biases toward them as well. There was a time when obesity, race, and gender biases were socially and legally acceptable. Decades later, weight indifference is still very much alive and tolerated. Overweight individuals are frequently stereotyped as lazy, low performers, and slobs. These only encourage the belief that if a person is thin, they are considered smarter, more energetic, and beautiful. Moreover, to be fat or even a large person is not acceptable. This is astounding

13

because more than 65% of the American population is overweight or obese.

Being a nurse for many years, I personally witnessed weight indifferences in the educational environment, workplace, and health care setting. This often resulted in unfair hiring practices, poor access to healthcare, and educational discouragement. At one time, overweight people were found to be paid fewer wages than thinner co-workers are. In some health care settings, overweight people were put into the same category as mental health patients, addicts, or alcoholics. Nurses often complained about taking care of obese patients and viewed them as repulsive. Not this nurse, of course. Today, there still exist no clear federal laws to protect the obese population from discrimination or other indifferences, but I suspect, like the need to address bullying, it will someday gain national attention.

Wait! I'm African American, so shouldn't I have a bodacious body with plenty of back? Not necessarily. Although my parents are of African descent, my mother's Creole ancestors descended from the colonial settlers in Louisiana, especially those of French and Spanish descent. So, without a doubt, our ethnic and cultural differences play a major role in the issues we face regarding weight, body shapes, and even our mindset regarding how these influence or do not influence our lives. Not being able to choose our shape limits our control over what we have to work with. There's not much junk in this trunk! My legs may be skinny, but they are cute and shapely. They are in proportion to my narrow hips and medium-size knockers. I've always been a Size 3-4, even when I did gain weight. So why did I hate my shape all those years? Because it was hard to find clothes to fit me nicely. They either fit in the waist or were too baggy in the hips and butt, or the opposite. I always had my clothes altered. However, it wasn't until after I discovered how exercising and strength training could sculpt and tone my body that I began to feel better about how I look. As mentioned earlier, genetics, metabolism, and hormones ultimately design our physical structure, so why battle with the inevitable? I choose to be happy and content with how I view myself. Now let's take a closer look at how culture and ancestry further influence our overall shape and physical appearance. Let's start by looking at five different ethnic and cultural groups living right here all around us.

How Does My Culture Affect My Shape?

Latin Women

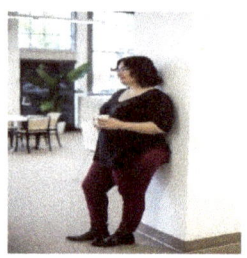

Photo by All Go App

Latin Culture consists of people from various parts of the Americas, such as Spain, Mexico, Central America, South America, and some Caribbean countries, and have a high presence in the United States. Many are referred to as Hispanic. The banana shape, also known as the rectangle shape, can be predominantly found in this ethnic group. Hispanic women tend to be short stature with thick bones and muscles, wide hips, and thick legs. These physical features can be seen in half of the Hispanic women in the United States today. Unfortunately, the Hispanic cultures have a particularly high prevalence of being overweight and obese; tied intimately to diet and behavioral attitudes toward weight loss and exercise.

Various studies have found that many Hispanic women believe that being plump is associated with being healthy. In addition, Hispanic women have been found to have lower body self-esteem than other ethnic groups and are not particularly interested in restricting their dietary intake. Their self-esteem is lower than both Caucasian and African American women. I did not know this.

The motivation for many of my Hispanic clients was to become healthier rather than to work on the shape and size of their bodies. One study found that the three major reasons why Hispanic women rarely exercised were; there was no time for exercising after taking care of the family, they were discouraged because family members who were active and presumed healthy had died anyway, and many felt that they were naturally healthy and didn't need to exercise or watch their food intake. Not only was I born and raised in a predominately-Hispanic community; I also married a very traditional Hispanic man. Our daughter is, of course, is biracial, and even though I think it's the best of both worlds she has to balance both cultural lifestyles and genetics.

Because culture is so intimately tied to nutrition, the first line of defense is to understand attitudes toward food since food often bond families and communities. The Mexican American diet is very rich in a variety of complex carbohydrates and fat that is unfortunately associated with obesity and chronic health conditions such as diabetes, cardiovascular disease, hypertension, and osteoporosis. For many years, I enjoyed these tasty dishes until I came to realize how high the fat, cholesterol, and sodium contents actually were and the long-term effects on the body. I still treat myself to a wonderful plate of enchiladas, beans, and rice, but only occasionally.

The overall physical activity level for many Hispanic women is commonly stifled due to being overweight and inactive. This is not isolated to just exercising but includes having sex, walking, gardening, and in some cases, normal activities of daily living. Check out these interesting responses from a study that asked women of various ethnic groups to identify their level of physical activity. Out of close to 300 women, 12% of Hispanic women reported that they don't exercise and do not plan to and the remaining 88% was a mixture of women that started and then stopped or who only occasionally workout. Amazing!

African American Women

Photo by Obi Onyeador

Women in this ethnic group are celebrated for their big BACK side. Yes, "baby got back." Well, not this baby. I was skipped when this was handed out. A nice gentleman once told me that I had other assets. That was putting it gently. I've heard so many women talk about how they lost their girlish hourglass figure, some not far from still being girls themselves. Little did they know that with being knowledgeable about their body and weight tendencies, they could have held on to or still have it, or some nice version of it.

The landscape for this group is the hourglass shape with various moderations, and a whole lot of cultural influence kicked in. Remember, this is my cultural heritage, and I have three sisters with different shapes and metabolisms, so I speak with some firsthand knowledge. African American women have the highest rate of being overweight and obese compared to other groups in the United States, 4 out of 5 to be exact, and 78% of black women in all of America. This puts these women at serious risk for developing hypertension (high blood pressure, the silent killer) and different cancers. The traditional African American diet, also known as "soul food," is rooted in the southern United States.

Lower socioeconomic conditions provided very little in the way of nutrition and healthy food. The meals consisted mostly of fried, breaded, and starchy foods with a variety of beef, pork, and grains such as grits, cornbread, biscuits, and macaroni with loads of cheese. These foods are extremely high in fat, cholesterol, and sodium. Fortunately, along with the not-so-good foods is an array of healthy leafy vegetables, such as collard, mustard, turnip greens, dried beans, and potatoes, which are high in protein. Among African Americans, the growing rate of Type 2 diabetes is an astounding 1.6 times higher than that of the United States population.

The acceptance and encouragement of being a full-figured black woman have taken on super-sized proportions. This is further perpetuated through images in magazines, music videos, and television, which feature black women with voluptuous butts, hips, and curves. Being "fabulous and thick" now may be in, but can ultimately lead to an unhealthy lifestyle and chronic health conditions later. For many years, I have always envied women who had it going on like this. When I was growing up, the wise older ladies in my family told me I wouldn't look like a skeleton forever. They said it would be in my twenties when my body would start to take some kind of shape, and then it was after I had a baby. So, I had three and no change. Finally, I was assured I would develop at least some hips when I reached my thirties, then forties. Well, I am passed that, and my Beyoncé body never showed up. It was never going to happen. I have since come to love my small size and shape, and I celebrate being healthy and active. I was so happy when I saw Kerry Washington play Olivia Pope in Scandal. She looks awesome with her cute, shapely, petite figure.

Studies have shown that African American women tend to be more satisfied with their bodies than other ethnic groups. They are more accepting of oversized and bulky body shapes and is generally not concerned with or learning about ideal body size and weight. Many claimed to have never been criticized for being overweight from close friends or relatives. And the typical thin ideal model image is of little importance for the women of color. Some even go as far as to attribute being overweight to God's plan for them. Others blame the stress of having to be a strong independent black woman, family association, aging, and the pressure of being expected to eat "soul food." If these obstacles aren't enough, African American men have never been shy about advertising how they prefer the fuller, curvier shape to a petite size, (that would be me, their loss).

When it comes to participating in various exercises, primarily cardio, many African American women avoid it like the plague and cite the inability to maintain their hairstyle. I said many, not all. One study revealed that over 40% of black women said that they absolutely did not exercise because of their hair, even though they understood the importance of being active. I can truly testify to this because I can't count the times, I wrecked my time-consuming (3-5 hours) and expensive hairstyles by going to the gym to only sweat it out. So, I had a standing rule not to work out for a while after visiting the beauty salon. Our naturally thick kinky curls are far from the wash-and-wear styles. Therefore, we resort to chemical relaxers and/or heat to get that beautiful straight look that can cause the hair to become damaged and fragile. To avoid adding insult to injury with sweating out the fresh "do," which requires frequent shampooing, many black women won't even consider it. I don't know how true it is, but, in addition to not wanting to mess up our hair, it is believed that women of color associate working out as a "man- thing."

21

Some good news is that I have been noticing more and more products on the market that offer sweat-absorbent hair wraps and bands that help to preserve the straightened texture and allow women to participate in more exercise routines. Hair weaving and braids are an excellent option. Speaking from experience, it is so difficult to have to choose between your hair and your health. I have always loved wearing wigs for their convenience, style, and versatility, and after losing my hair following chemotherapy, I fell more in love with them. Now I alternate between cute all-natural short hairstyles and some of the most beautifully fashioned wigs I've ever seen. Both of which allow me to work out daily and enjoy the Jacuzzi and sauna. It is also suggested that African American women don't lose as much weight as Caucasian women who engage in the same weight-loss interventions. Therefore, making it even more crucial to become health-conscious and engage in a regular exercise program. So, get busy!

Caucasian Women

Photo by Jose Martinez

The Western cultured Caucasian woman comes in many shapes and sizes. But, the most desirable shape was, and to some extent and still is, the stereotyped "skinny girl" look. Being slender and physically attractive has been generally associated with youth, happiness, and success, and who doesn't want that?

Cultural expectations and idealizations have had the most profound effect on our Caucasian sisters. Traditionally, the "perfect" women was portrayed as the thin, tall, zero-size supermodel type, creating an obsession to have the perfect body. Over the years, the lust after the ideal body image has often led to a variety of eating disorders and even death in some cases.

According to some studies, Caucasian women have also been found to have the most negative body image, lower self-esteem, and preference to be thinner than the recommended weight for their age and height, when compared to Black or Hispanic women. Also, these views of the ideal body weight have been responsible for creating a zero-tolerance for the slightest weight gain, resulting in a multibillion-dollar weight loss industry. Thanks to the cosmetic surgery craze, we are seeing less and less of the flat butts and itty-bitty breasts these women have been associated with in the past.

23

When it comes to exercise, these women take the cake. I have been to gyms and classes on cruise ships, tropical islands, and many other vacation spots, and there has never failed to be a dedicated group taking classes, on the treadmills, elliptical machines, aqua aerobics, and other fun aerobic classes. They do not hesitate to sign up for a weight loss program or get the fat sucked right out of them. The wash and go hair texture is a major plus, and it is believed that Caucasian women lose approximately seven pounds more weight than African American women on the same diet and weight loss regiments. This is apparently due to a higher resting metabolism and energy level.

Asian Women

Photo by Aexandra Lammerink

Women in this culture tend to be petite in size, straight with angular body shape. Not only does genetics play a big role in their size, but also culture and diet. In the ancient Chinese dynasties, women starved themselves to stay thin in order to receive royal favor. They ultimately appeared frail and extremely thin, anorexic. This thin body ideal has carried over into the Asian American culture and has a large influence on how these women feel about their size and shape. Did you know that many Asian women were known to be more obsessed with thinness than white women? I didn't. And although different types of foods vary among the different Asian traditions, meals consist mostly of vegetables, fish, grains, tofu, and fruit. Many Asian women choose to practice vegetarianism. This healthier and less fattening cuisine is becoming more popular among western Americans.

Body image among Asian American Women varies greatly. Some studies resulted in Asian American women having a negative self-image, while others found them to have a positive body image. This is due largely to the variety of ethnicities of Asian women, including Chinese, Japanese, Korean, and Vietnamese women. Asian women who identify with the Asian culture tend to adopt a thinner body image, whereas Asian women who identify with the American culture will favor a thicker body ideal. Much like the type of cuisines associated with each Asian culture, ideas, and behaviors regarding exercise and physical activity vary also, but are somewhat similar.

Asian women have been thought of as having a "dainty approach" to exercising. In some East Asian countries like China, Japan, and Taiwan, physical activities and exercise are centered on more traditional practices such as walking, bike riding, and the martial arts, mainly for health and enjoyment versus weight and fitness. A leisurely stroll on the treadmill, followed by a facial or other beauty treatment, still was considered a well-balanced workout; I love it. This practice, along with the traditionally healthy diet, resulted in a long and happy life. When Asians migrated to the Western World, they were quickly introduced to this fast-paced lifestyle with its hectic schedules, bad eating habits, and eventually, poor health. Once believed to be a culture with longevity for life, is now plagued with the same chronic diseases, other cultures are battling. I remember only seeing a small number of Asian women in the gyms. However, this has changed considerably because of the variety of energetic aerobic workouts now available. Looking forward to seeing you in Zumba.

SECTION TWO

What If I Don't Like My Shape?

Many of us women have spent the majority of our lives wanting to have a different body. Over the years, my shape has caused me varying degrees of anxiety. I was either too thin, too fat around the middle, or both. I had no shame in wearing padded bras and underwear that gave me the curves I didn't naturally possess. And, when breast implants became popular in the eighties, I was first in line. If it was going to alter this body and make me gorgeous, I wanted it. Plus, it didn't hurt that I worked for a plastic surgeon. In addition to my puny figure, I wished I was taller with straight white teeth and had naturally long and beautiful hair, but these details were not encoded in my gene pool. Over the years, I have actually had women tell me they wish their arms were more defined like mine or had my strength, stamina, and endurance. I always relish these types of compliments because they make me feel good to know that others admire me for just the way I am. Today I embraced what I was born with, made it work, and keep it moving.

As a cosmetic surgical nurse, I saw so many women and men seeking procedures to change the way they looked. They sought smaller noses, rounder eyes, larger penises, and more. Some came back over and over again. And how many times have we seen how addictive plastic surgery can become, many botched.

Historically, it was the corset, the tighter, the better, and padded bras that were the lifesavers for women to achieve their tiny waist size and plumb breast. Today with access and excess of cosmetic surgeries, treatments and other procedures, we can permanently or even temporarily alter our look and shape in an instant. That's the beauty of it. Let's take a quick look at just a few of the most popular ways to reshape your body.

Breast Implants

Yes, these girls can be artificially increased with implants or surgically reduced. Padded bras and removable prosthetics are still in and a great way to see how potential changes will look before taking the plunge. Breast implants have been around since the late nineteenth century, so this is not a new phenomenon, just one that has been perfected over the years. It was initially performed to correct breast asymmetry after tumor removal and other post-surgical breast procedures, and the fillers used often consisted of various types of materials like wax, rubber, and sponges, often leading to disastrous results. Today, silicone, saline, and donor tissues are used to achieve the same but better and safer results. The type of breast implant device and filler materials selected is highly dependent on a female's or male's personal preference.

I still run into plenty of women of all ages who are still not familiar with the aesthetic implication of breast implants. Simply put, it is a prosthesis that simulates the shape and feel of a natural breast. It can change the size, form, and shape of the breast. It was a godsend for cancer patients like me who underwent a bilateral mastectomy and breast reconstruction, allowing us to to feel whole again. For the small-breasted women who wanted to join the bodacious tah-tahs club, it was a miracle, and for the male-to-female transgender, it is a dream come true.

Pectoral Implants

Some women and most men have taken advantage of these types of implants to enhance the lines of their chests and instill a sense of self-confidence. Outside of being an option for injury and reconstruction, they are purely for cosmetic desires. The chest implants are made of solid silicone, but are still very soft and flexible, so when touched they feel and look like the real deal. These come in different shapes and sizes and are placed behind the chest muscles.

Calf Implants (Calf Augmentation)

We don't hear about this much in our everyday environment, but it is a very popular procedure that can create fullness in the lower leg area. Like many of the procedures mentioned here, both men and women seek out these legs reshaping implants. If I were rich, I'd have some too, trust me.

Tummy Tuck

Whoever thought of this wonderful procedure is a genius. The surgical name for a tummy tuck is known as abdominoplasty and involves removing excess fat and skin from the abdominal area, restoring a smoother and firmer waist. I've seen this done on multiple occasions for both men and women, and the results have been a beautifully flat and well-toned abdomen. When this cannot be achieved through traditional exercise and weight loss methods, this is a great option. This is not just for overweight people, even those with normal body weight and are unhappy with a protruding, saggy, or loose abdomen, brought on by the aging process, heredity, pregnancy, other abdominal surgeries and fluctuations in weight gain and loss. As an added bonus, unattractive stretch marks and other scars can be greatly improved or even removed if located in the same area. With any weight loss or body reshaping process, regular exercise can not only maintain your awesome new look but enhance it by toning and strengthening the muscles that support it. Check out some before and after pictures online if you haven't already, you will be amazed.

Butt Lift

Talk about exciting; as I mentioned earlier, I've only been able to dream of what a shapely derriere on me would look and feel like. This procedure surgically lifts drooping buttocks and thighs, creating a beautiful full-looking hinny. This involves removing the skin and tightening at the incision line to lift and shape the butt. The results? Super gratifying

The buttock padding is puckered and stitched in place to give it more projection and bump. This can make the behind appear at least ten years younger. This procedure can be done at the same time as the tummy tuck, giving you that gorgeous "Rump Roast" and a flat belly. Also, depending on your personal preference, buttock implants come in a variety of sizes and shapes to choose from. These are placed on top or under the muscle, with the incision hidden between the buttocks for a flawless appearance.

If any of this seems a little extreme, then don't worry, excess fat can be suctioned from another part on your body, usually the abdomen, and easily injected into the buttocks, hence the Brazilian Butt Lift.

Liposuction

Lipoblast, also known as liposuction, is a surgical procedure that removes fat from many different parts of the body. Personally, I like to think of it as "fat modeling," sounds more intriguing. Although originating in France as early as 1926, it did not become popular until the 1960s. Advanced technology has improved the technique, resulting in less blood loss, discomfort, and risk. These suborn fat cells can be removed from the thighs, abdomen, buttocks, arms, and back. So, here's how it is performed; the fat is literally sucked out with a hollow tube or cannula. The specific technique and amount of fat removed is based upon individual circumstances and desires. Recovery time is short, and pain is minimal. Beware, the fat can return without maintaining a good exercise and nutritional program

Total Body Lift

The total body lift is, well totally amazing. What an incredible transformation or metamorphosis from head to toe. Multiple areas on the body are literally nipped, tucked, and suctioned. Two former co-workers had this procedure, and they looked like they had a body transplant. When I say body lift, I mean body lift, abdomen, thighs, back, tummy, arms, breast, and buttocks, all in one swoop. This took more discipline and commitment than I can ever imagine. When you are hell-bound and determined, nothing can stop you. And, they were!

Body Shapewear

For those of you who do not dare to venture into the world of plastic surgery, don't fret. The invention of the body shaper is here to save the day. Whether you want to achieve a flatter tummy, fuller breast, firmer thighs, or shapelier butt, there's a style for you. Just ask the visionary and billionaire, inventor of Spanx Shapewear.

Body shapers are wonderful for creating smoother lines, underpants, dresses, and normal everyday clothes. I've seen women and men wear them under their workout clothes. Hey, why not? Many are comfortable, slimming, and sexy and will give you curves in all the right places. I wouldn't do too much cardio in them, but a few Big Macs (exercise to work the butt) and some bend over rows might work better than an online dating service if that's your thing, didn't work for me.

As a nurse and personal trainer, I am a big proponent of reshaping the body naturally through healthy eating, body sculpting, and good old-fashioned cardio exercises. Changing your body, no matter what shape, can give you a great sense of control and satisfaction over so many other areas in your life. What you see on the scale does not have to reflect how you feel and ultimately look with or without clothes on. You can be a size 2 or 22 and be in the best shape of your life. So, the hell with the rest and get addicted to the feeling and looking good.

Many of us women have spent the majority of our lives wanting to have a different body. I wish I was taller with straight white teeth, naturally long and beautiful hair, but this detail was not encoded in my gene pool. So, I embrace what I was born with and make it happen. I have actually had women tell me they wish their arms and shoulders were more shaped like mine. I always

33

relished in these types of compliments because it makes me feel good to know that others admire me for just the way I am.

Today, there are many cosmetic options available from temporary to permanent, so it just boils down to whatever makes your boat float for a happier you.

SECTION THREE

Principles to Jump Start A New You

1. Wear the Right Clothes for Your Shape:

Choosing the right clothes for your shape, size, and comfort is so important to staying emotionally balanced when it comes to feeling good about yourself. Height and even weight should not influence how you shop for clothes, but rather what your unique shape is. There are many great articles on the do's and don'ts of choosing the right clothes to flatter your best assets. Here are some good things to keep in mind the next time you want to find that special outfit.

- If you lean toward the pear shape persuasion, then find clothes that accentuate your waist and arms while slimming down the appearance of the hips and round bottom. Wide dresses, skirts, and pants will balance those hippy hips. Kim Kardashian West has no problem in this area.

- When your best asset is your gorgeous legs, and your chest and shoulders are in wider proportion, dress to soften the upper body with cool colors and clothes that slim the waistline. This shape helped Demi Moore kick ass in GI Jane and made her look stunning next to Ashton.

- Create curves for a slender body shape by wearing clothes that show off the arms and legs. For me, that would be ruffles, long blouses, and jackets that flair at the waist. Try layering, especially with flowing collars and bright colors to add more dimension. Works for me every time. Remember Hilary Swank in Million Dollar Baby?

- A woman with a big and beautiful apple shape will do well to dress so that her waist appear slimmer and the legs emphasized, think Jennifer Hudson, and you will see the epitome of how to flaunt this shape.

- Well, this is my all-time favorite, the magnificent hourglass shape. Halle Berry and I have nothing in common here. Magnify these curves with any style clothing that makes your waist look tiny and the top and bottom look fabulous.

As you can see with any figure, if it lifts, shapes, or is slimming; you've got it going on.

2. Empower Thy Self:

I can't think of anything that's more sustaining in life. If it wasn't for the concept of self-empowerment or self-motivation, I truly don't know where I would be. Earnest Hemmingway put it best, "life breaks people, and in the broken places, you will find the strong" I added that you would also find the weak and the ones that are no longer here. How profound is that? It's inevitable, there will be so many trials and tribulations in life, and we can only pray that each one makes us better and stronger. For whatever crazy reason, it seems to be human nature to crave all the things that are not healthy. They may be good to us, but they are certainly not good for us.

Over the years, I have had so many ridiculous binges it's not even funny, and always found the perfect excuse, "I'm on vacation and I am going to eat and drink until times get better" or "oh what the hell, I'll work it off later." However, later never came, and the older I got, the harder it was to work it off and the longer it took. I started replacing these self-defeating ideas and behaviors with ones that I could pat myself on the back for.

I could read all the self-help books in the world, which I love, but the power had to come from within, and it needed to cover every aspect of my physical, emotional, mental, spiritual and

37

financial wellbeing. When one of these crucial areas is out of balance in my life, I am one twisted sister. So, what did I do? I committed myself to daily devotionals and positive affirmations. I countered every negative thought or word with a positive one and immediately forgave myself for being human. I wrote down every positive thought-provoking quote, watched only uplifting and encouraging movies, and started reading testimonies and memoirs of how other strong men and women overcame their toughest challenges to succeed. It got creative juices flowing, I didn't even know I had, and I love every minute of it.

This practice not only helped to curtail stress, find peace of mind, and get into great physical shape, but it inspired the writing of this book and two other articles for Spry Magazine and Press Enterprise Newspaper about health and wellness.

3. Get Connected:

Find like-minded people to connect with. This is motivating and fun even if it's going to a workout class. I love watching others working out and getting their sweat on. I'm especially motivated by those that are disabled, recovering from an injury or simply one of our esteemed senior. They "work it like nobody's watching," and I never miss an opportunity to tell them to keep up the great work. The smiles on their faces are priceless.

Exercising to videos at home or at work is not obsolete. I started out with Jane Fonda, Denise Austin, and one of my favorites, Billy Blank's Tae Bo, just to name a few. They were great for getting that workout in when I didn't have time to get to the gym between working at the hospital and taking care of the family. Today, there are thousands to choose from, all easily accessible from the cell phone, tablets and computer. One could literally watch a video and workout anywhere in the world. How about that for no more excuses? As to which ones I highly recommend, all of them. More realistically, go with the ones that meet your specific fitness level and don't forget to have fun, fun, fun.

4. Express Yourself:

Find the right style of clothing that's appropriate for your body shape. For example, leggings are not a respecter of all. That's all I'm going to say about that. Choosing the right style of clothes for your shape eases a lot of frustration out of shopping. Have you ever in your entire life bought a dress, blouse, pants, or God forbid, a workout outfit that looks horrible on you once you got it home? And that was after trying it on in the store or maybe not. I've done it a million times, and right now, I have clothes in my closet with the tags still on them because I will never go out of the house looking like Olive Oil. Like you, I bought them because they looked cute on the mannequin, or perhaps I had a break in reality and thought that someday I would have a completely new body. Whatever the case, they didn't fit my unique shape. Once you determine your body shape, then you can begin to shop and create special looks just for you. Wearing the right clothes can actually make you look slimmer in certain desired areas and heftier in others; I'll have some of the latter, please.

5. Try Something New:

If your exercise routine starts to become mundane and boring, don't be afraid to mix it up and try something new. For example, just working out on the treadmill or elliptical machine can become dull and less exciting after a while. When this happens, you may have the tendency to get distracted and find excuses not to do it. Many exercise classes are designed to accommodate all exercise levels, so you can make it as high or low impact as you want, and trust me no one will even notice.

If your workout routine consists mostly of cardio exercises, then add a strength training class that uses weights, bands, and other ways to build your muscles. Try yoga to transform your body and mind, Pilates to condition the body and build strength, flexibility, and endurance. Don't just marvel at an aqua aerobics class next time, dive in, it's amazing. Take it outside for some power walking, tennis classes, and now popular Pickleball, no, the ball isn't shaped like a pickle. Challenging the body with a variety of moves works different muscle groups and increases your fitness level, producing better results.

My personal fitness régime consists of a diverse mix of strength training, kickboxing, Zumba, spinning, hiking, bike riding, jogging, power walking, jump roping, jumping jacks, bowling, aqua aerobics, and of course my own Home Grown Park Circuit Routine. I enjoyed a lot of these activities with my fellow fitness instructor Bill the "Zumba King," and after his untimely death, it's what helped me to carry on both physically and psychologically. There are so many options to choose from, and not enough reasons not to. Don't forget to consult your personal health care team before deciding to become the next Wonder Woman.

6. Love the Skin You're In:

We live in our skin, so we may as well just settle back and get comfortable if you haven't already. Develop an attitude of working with what you got, what you were born with, and how you need to manage it. I personally know this is easier said than done, especially being surrounded by so many idealistic images. Just think that if you had a personal make-up artist, chef, hairstylist, and personal trainer at your beck and call, you would look fabulous all the time, too. However, working a nine-to-five and running a household is not quite the same.

When you look at the women in the mirror, give her a compliment and an encouraging word. I was impressed to see hundreds of posted notes with varying affirmations and empowering thoughts on one client's wall and mirror. Another would create a vision board with positive sayings and/or pictures of health and fitness. Over time, reminding yourself of your wonderful qualities will reinforce a positive attitude toward how you perceive and accept yourself for who you really are, not some fantasy. So, Do You and Keep It Real!

7. Your Best Asset:

This seems to be a concept that most of the women and men I've met on this journey tend not to focus on. And it's one of the first questions I always pose before a training session. I am very passionate about this subject because it is truly where the rubber meets the road. So many people get so caught up in the latest diet craze that they overlook the importance of being fit and healthy. Personal trainers are not magicians and cannot transform an apple shape into an hourglass shape as much as we would like to. It's just not going to happen, and that's why it's so important that men and women who decide to commit to a workout routine are realistic about their short and long-term goals. What's your best asset, and what part of your body will enhance it? Ok, let's start there and add some cardio and strength training, and the rest will follow. Stop terrorizing yourself with delusions of grandeur and be the best that you can be or become. Love you regardless of what shape or size you are, they don't call it big and beautiful for nothing. Focus on the possibilities and not the problem.

8. Maintain Balance

One must nurture every aspect of their lifestyle in order to achieve a state of health and wellness. This requires balanced physically, emotionally, spiritually, intellectually, socially, and environmentally. Let's briefly consider several of these:

> ➢ **Physical Balance** is how we care for our bodies in several ways. For example, eating a well-balanced diet, getting regular exercise, and being a self-advocate when it comes to regular medical and dental check-ups. I like to think of it as being an ambassador for our well-being. If I didn't seek medical care immediately after finding the lump in my breast, I might not have had the opportunity to finish this book.

> ➢ **Emotional Balance** is what helped me to deal with the shock of a cancer diagnosis and every other emotional encounter in my life. Some days were a lot better than others, but it was how quickly I was able to regroup, that was most important. Stress is a part of life, but remember there is good stress, and there is bad stress, but it is bad stress that we need good coping mechanisms to deal with. One of the wonderful benefits of staying physically active is that it helps produce the hormones and endorphins that make us feel happy and well.

> ➢ **Spiritual Balance** is exactly what that means to you and how you tap into your sense of purpose and meaning in this life. Whatever form it takes whether tangible or non-tangible, it should bring you "Love, Peace, and Joy." This quote is from the 80's dance show, Love Train. Think about it, they loved hearing and dancing to the music because it brought them happiness and a sense of

connection that they could carry to other areas of their lives. As a young girl, I always dreamed of being on that show, and even now, the thought of it makes me happy.

➤ **Intellectual Balance** is so important to keep the mind interactive and strong. I consider myself a professional student because I am always learning something new. I decided to take some nutritional and creative writing classes at the local community college after I retired. Being around so much knowledge and young minds was amazing. I decided to take a wig making certification course, and now I can make a variety of personal and custom wigs. Whatever your forte is, be it reading, attending seminars, taking classes, or engaging in stimulating conversation, it's all good.

➤ **Benefits of Staying Active** is good for you. There are so many ways to accomplish this. Believe it or not, any amount of activity is better than none at all. Here are a few of these benefits to think about the next time exercising crosses your mind:

- Increase Energy (Get Up and Go)
- Reduced Risk for Cardiovascular Disease (Healthy Heart)
- Prevents Bone Loss (Strong Bones)
- Improves Mood or Feeling of Well-Being (Powerful Antidepressant)
- Slows the Aging Process (Fountain of Youth)
- Better Sleep (Sweet Dreams)

With benefits like these, how can you go wrong? When I took my Nutrition and Fitness class, it was right next to the track. So, I would arrive an hour before class to walk/run and stretch. Not only was it great to be outside in that fresh morning air with the beautiful mountains as a backdrop, but it was awesome to see so many men and women of all ages out there. I would walk/jog between the light poles around the track several times, and that was challenging, in twelve weeks, I was jogging around five times nonstop. When I went to class, I felt exhilarated and energized. One of the hardest things to do when I'm feeling blue or melancholy is to work out. I have literally driven up to the front of the gym and sped off like a criminal fleeing the scene of a crime. Later it made me laugh, and then I realized that if I just don't think about going and just go, I would leave feeling ten times better. Get up and get busy.

SECTION FOUR

How Does My Body Really Work?

Photo courtesy of Delbra Woodard

Teaching Anatomy and Physiology always amazed me at how wonderfully made the human body is. This really helped my students understand and appreciate how well the body functions to preserve health and life. So before starting any exercise program, it is important to know how the body works to benefit physical activity. Here's your quick course. First and foremost, the skeletal system provides movement of all our bones as well as protects the internal organs. Without it, we would resemble a human jellyfish. That's why it's so extremely important to keep them healthy and strong. Loss of bone mass and strength is inevitable with age, but regular exercise can slow the process, prevent bone loss, and keep us walking upright versus humped over. Next, we have what's connected to the bones, the muscles.

The physical movement of the skeletal system is created by approximately 600 muscles in the human body. This is a lot of force, and we use much of it for everyday living. When it comes to performing an exercise, we need good strength and endurance of our muscles. Good strong muscles and bones are essential in preventing injury and joint, and back pain. There are three types of muscle movements: isotonic, isometric, and isokinetic. Isotonic is the movement that occurs at the joint and is the most common and preferred movement for regular exercise. A good example of isotonic exercise would be lifting a barbell. Isometric is muscular tension with no movement, and isokinetic movement involves action that is performed at a constant speed and usually involves a machine. Regular exercise will improve muscular strength and endurance, and you can take that to the bank.

Should My Heart Beat This Fast?

Photo by Christen LeCorte

Good cardiovascular (heart and blood vessels) endurance is paramount to establishing a good exercise program and being successful at it. Getting out of breath while climbing a flight of stairs is what convinced me to quit smoking cigarettes. This system allows us to perform activities like brisk walking, jogging, swimming, or cycling over a period of time while reaping the benefits of losing weight, reducing the risk of disease, and improving our lives overall. Although having a strong heart and blood vessels are important, they would be severely compromised without a healthy respiratory system. This is the ability to breathe in good air and expel waste from our bodies through our lungs. The heart and the lungs work harmoniously together so that we are able to perform the physical demands necessary for exercise and activities of our daily living.

This is where the term aerobic exercise comes from and is simply a prolonged exercise that utilizes the breakdown of food along with oxygen to produce the energy or fuel we need to work out. On the other hand, anaerobic exercise does not use oxygen for energy and usually occurs during short high-intensity type exercises such as isolated leg exercises or short distance running. This is when you feel the burn produced by the buildup of lactic acid. The cardiorespiratory system is an intricate and complex system that helps us to experience a full and healthy life if we are willing to take the time to nurture and take advantage of all the health-related benefits it provides, so pump it up.

Is Exercise on My List of New Year's Resolutions?

Photo by Ravim Noga

After the New Year, it is inevitable that boatloads of men and women will show up at the gym to fulfill one of the most aborted New Year's resolutions ever made. It's kind of a running joke at the gym to see how many disappear by just the third week in January. The stragglers usually make it to around mid-March, and they are never to be seen again until the next year. Although this may seem funny, it is really quite sad. The number one reason why so many people fail is unrealistic expectations, coupled with not being prepared. According to one study, it takes about 60 days to develop a habit, and from what I see, less than a week to drop one. Right after the first of the year, I saw a couple working out together in their matching pajamas; it was actually cute. They weren't going to let anything get in their way of starting off their New Year right. I was impressed, once I got over the shock. So here are some worthwhile steps to consider before taking that leap of faith and going to the gym for the first time or after a long sabbatical.

Step 1: Set Realistic Goals- These should consist of both short-term and long-term goals. Take into consideration your physical condition, fitness level, and what type of exercise excites you. This will help motivate you and not overwhelm you. Exercising should be fun and something you look forward to, not dread.

Step 2: Choose the Right Activities-There are so many to choose from if you enjoy cardio more than strength training than make that the focus of your work out. For example, swimming, running, cycling, treadmill, elliptical, and countless others are excellent for cardiorespiratory fitness. The same would be true if you prefer more toning than strength training. Just remember to remain balanced and include activities that work the whole body.

Step 3: Discover the FIT Principle- This stand for frequency, intensity, and time of your exercise session. An example would be working out 2 to 3 times a week with moderate intensity for a duration of 35 minutes. Your routine can be designed in a variety of different ways to best fit your personal workout style. A personal trainer can be a lifesaver in helping to develop these basic principles. I share several stories in the Standing Ovations Section.

Does Overweight Mean I'm Obese?

Photo by All Go App

Some people have more or less body weight than others. I see large sized people at the gym who appear very healthy. Being paper-thin and a gym rat doesn't necessarily mean a person is healthy. A contributing factor to being unhealthy is the amount of fat we carry, seen and unseen. Fat can be hidden around the internal organs and other places. Therefore, a percentage of the total body composition of fat and free fat in the body is necessary to determine a healthy body weight. In other words, the percentage of body fat a person has determines if they are obese, overweight, or at a desirable weight. Please don't be misled by thinking that extra love handles are great to hold on to. Because being overweight and having a high percentage of body fat has been linked to multiple chronic diseases such as heart disease, diabetes, and others. On the flip side, having an extremely low percentage of body fat can be just as serious.

I truly love statistics and must mention that approximately 54% of adults and children are obese. I think one of the major factors, outside of poor diet and inactivity, is not understanding how subtle weight gain can be over a period of years. This is referred to as "creeping obesity. Yes, our body metabolism slows, and our body shape softens with age, but that does not mean we can't or shouldn't be a healthy weight along the way. I was shocked to learn that just drinking one soda a day can add up to 15 extra pounds a year. That's why a former co-worker who came to work every morning with a supersized Coke, looked like Tugboat Annie, sorry, but it's true. Too bad, because I love me some Coke also. Don't be fooled by diet sodas, studies have shown that some people do gain a significant amount of belly fat over time.

BMI (Body Mass Index) Calculation

There are various ways to determine your body mass index; however, one of the simplest ways I found is to use your handy phone calculator and follow these steps:

BMI = Height (in inches) X Height (in inches), now divide your weight by the number of inches previously calculated. Next, multiply this number by 705. For example, Karen weighs 132 lbs. and is 5 feet 7 inches Karen's BMI =   Step 1. 67 (inches) x 67(inches) = 4,489

Step 2. 132 lbs. divided by 4,489 = 0.029

Step 3. 0.029 X 705 = 20.73 BMI

According to the National Institutes of Health (NIH), a BMI between 19 and 24.9 is considered a healthy range. An elevated BMI above this range significantly increases the risk of health-related diseases and untimely death. When it comes to maintaining a healthy weight and living an active lifestyle, it's critical to the longevity of our lives. I would always try to encourage and motivate my clients by telling them that by making one positive change in their lifestyle could potentially afford them more time to spend with their children and/or grandchildren. Who wouldn't want to enjoy more time on this earth, especially if by our positive behaviors and lifestyle changes, we could influence this?

I think this is an appropriate time for me to share a very personal experience. Four years ago, today, a very close friend suffered a massive stroke. He had just celebrated his 70th birthday and was the youngest of five other siblings well into their eighties. He always joked that he was going to live to be 90 like his Portuguese ancestors, and quite frankly, I believed him. The man lived like he had nine lives. Over the years, he survived a large benign neck mass, prostate cancer, a heart attack, and two brain surgeries for subdural hematomas after tripping over a parking curb. After his death, his eulogy captured all the wonderful and fun memories of his life, but the real story is that his lifestyle was a train wreck.

He was a family man with a long and lucrative career in the banking industry, did little to curtail his lifestyle of smoking, heavy drinking, and unhealthy diet. At some point, he quit smoking after many years, but he continued on his path of self-destruction until he reached the fifth and final of his nine lives. My point is that he didn't have to die so soon. The drinking and high-fat diet contributed to the development of his hypertension, high cholesterol, and, ultimately, Type 2 diabetes. He was discovered two days later in his favorite recliner, watching his favorite TV program and his favorite glass of red wine next to him. He forfeited those extra years he could have spent with the grandchildren he never got a chance to see. He looked much younger than his age, and we had just started a regular workout routine together. Sorry for the downer, but just another example that inspired me to help others get serious about being healthy. Oh, I forgot to mention that my friend didn't want to change; he actually said, "if the doctor told me I had to stop drinking, you may as well take me outside and put a bullet in my head." And there you have it, was it worth it?

This story was not about trying to scare you straight, but to create a subtle awareness of how we live, which affects how long we live.

SECTION FIVE

How Do I Avoid Conking Out?

If you ever took an aerobics class or simply climbed a flight of stairs and found yourself huffing and puffing, don't' panic, you are not dying. This is because your body is responding to the physical activity. The heart rate increases to ensure the body is getting the necessary oxygenated blood and other substances it needs for the job. Our breathing increases to not only deliver that good oxygen but also to rid the body of carbon dioxide. These responses are good and necessary for building stamina and endurance. Over time and with a regular routine, you will gradually improve. You will find yourself able to stay on the treadmill longer, getting through an aerobics class with ease or even walking or jogging longer as I did on the track. This is the time to high-five yourself because you hung in there to reap the positive benefits. Not only would your overall endurance improved, but your energy level will also increase. Take note of the tone and definition to those muscles that have been hiding for years. Have a coming-out party to celebrate.

Start your exercise routine with a warm-up and a cool-down session. This is important to prepare the body for the workout and then to return it to its regular functioning state. So, let's get with it:

Now Let's Stretch It Out

Be sure to include some mild and light stretching. Do this to warm the muscles and avoid injury. Overstretching cold muscles is no fun and can take months to heal. Stretching helps us to move our joints through their full range of motion without difficulty and helps to maintain flexibility, which is crucial for our everyday activities such as bending and lifting. Not only does stretching keep our joints healthy and mobile, but it can also prevent lower back pain and improve our posture. My routine consists of a combination of floor and machine stretching. It's important to maintain good posture when doing either of these, so if you are unsure of how to do these or if you are experiencing discomfort, don't hesitate to ask one of the friendly trainers at your gym for guidance, they will be happy to assist you. Here is a quick overview of different types of stretching:

- Static Stretching- This is the most desirable and effective stretching because it improves flexibility by stretching to the point of minimal discomfort and holding it for approximately 20 -30 seconds. Before and after a good workout, static stretching aids in reducing muscle stiffness and soreness. These can be performed practically anywhere, at home, work, and even in the car because no special equipment is needed.

- Dynamic Stretching- This type of stretching is good for many exercise programs and sports training and requires moving the joints through the full range of motion. Example: Walking Knee Lifts.

- Ballistic Stretching- Involves a fast and forceful bouncing movement. This type of stretching is less desirable for routine workouts because of the potential for injury. Example: Bouncing up and down while touching your toes.

- Proprioceptive Neuromuscular Facilitation (PNF) - Consist of a combination of stretching, contracting, and relaxing muscles. This is one of my favorites because it feels good to break up a long continuous stretch, it can be challenging, but definitely worth the effort.

Stretching will improve flexibility and enhance your exercise routine. I created a "10 To Win" stretch routine. When I first wake up every morning, I stand and stretch my arms, back, sides, and hamstrings for 10 seconds, followed by ten repetitions of lunges and sit-ups. It's a great way to start and/or finish your day. Happy Stretching.

Now Let's Warm-Up

Begin with about 5 to 10 minutes of light exercise and stretching. Suppose you are going to engage in aerobics exercise, then do some low-intensity movement similar to what you will be doing. For example, before I take Zumba, I walk on the treadmill or hop on the stair stepper machine to warm and loosen my muscles. Or I may hit the weight machines for a few sets of light weights (10-15 lbs.) with high repetitions before a Body Pump Class. The weight machines can be a great way to warm up before a workout.

Now Let's Work That Body

Make your workout your own. Someone else's routine may not fit your personal goals and desires. I strongly recommend designing a basic routine and then adding on exercises that you enjoy, and that is compatible with your fitness level. Over the years, I have created a smorgasbord of workout routines for others, and myself, but it really depends on personal goals and expected outcomes. Sometimes I stick with the same routine for weeks because it just feels right. Keep in mind that's its regular exercise at an intensity that will raise your heart rate for at least 30-45 minutes that will provide the greatest benefits.

One way to measure the intensity of a workout is to get the heart rate to a level that promotes burning calories and, ultimately, fat to lose weight if that is your goal. Try working out at 50% to

85% of your target heart rate, also known as the "aerobic or cardio zone." If you are just starting out, this range may be lower, between 50% and 65%. The calculation to determine your target heart rate can seem a little overwhelming at first, but really, it's quite simple. Kudos to technology because on most treadmills, elliptical, and cycling machines, the target heart rate is determined for you after entering your age and weight. Here is a formula if you want to do it yourself, perhaps while jogging or riding your bike.

Formula

1. 220 - age = Maximum Heart Rate (Max HR)

2. Subtract resting heart rate from the Max HR = Heart Rate Reserve (HRR)

3. Multiply HRR times desired intensity percentage (50-85%)

4. Add the resting heart rate

Example: If my resting heart rate was 70 (beats per minute) at 40 years old, and my training intensity is the 70% range: 220 - 40 = 180, 180-70 = 110, 110 x .70% = 77, 77 + 70 = 147, Bingo!

Determining your target heart rate now allows you to monitor the intensity of your workouts and rewards you with a big jolt of encouragement from knowing your efforts are not in vain; how cool is that?

Now Let's Cool Down

Now that you are feeling pumped up and ready for the world, it's time to bring your body back to its pre-workout state by performing some cool down stretching and slow movements. Unfortunately, I see too many people skip this important part of the workout routine. I kid you not; one evening, a friend called me to seek my advice about the fainting spell he had on the basketball court. He explained that after the game, he did what he would normally do, sit down, pack up, and head home. On this particular day, he hiked several miles before the game and just jumped right into it when he arrived on the court. This time after the game, he became dizzy and developed what he described as "tunnel vision." After 911 was called, he was hauled off to the emergency room. His heart and respiratory system needed to return to their normal state slowly. Abruptly stopping a workout causes blood to pool in the extremities and could possibly cause dizziness or a cardiac event. The cooldown also aids in decreasing muscle soreness, and that's always a good thing. These 10-15 minutes will be well worth it.

SECTION SIX

Now That I Got One Foot Off the Ground, What's Next?

Each person's motivation to stay healthy and active will come from a special place all of its own. Identifying what your true motivation for wanting to exercise will heavily influence your commitment and, ultimately, your success. For example, a former client started working out because she wanted to jump on the internet dating bandwagon. When most of the men she met had a good time with her and then rode off into the sunset, so did her motivation to work out. Exercise to stay healthy and fit, everything is "Gravy Train." There are more than enough hours in a week to squeeze in three 30-minute workouts to improve your life. If you are a workaholic, a soccer mom of five children, or a traveling nurse, you can find time to do some type of exercise, somewhere, and somehow. I always keep a record of what I accomplish during my exercise sessions in my daily planner. This helps me to not only stay motivated, but tracked my progress, Wow! I really impress myself sometimes with how far I've come after nine surgeries and twenty-four months of recovery after breast cancer. Check out some of the things that keep me motivated and moving.

- **Work Out with A Pooch-** When a puppy rescued me from the shelter, she became my regular exercise partner. We started out walking a couple of times a day, and before I knew it, we transitioned into jogging on the trail around the lake at the park. We fell in love with this routine, and I got into the best shape ever right before summer and swimsuit time.

- **Focus On How Your Body Responds-** Ask yourself: "How do my legs feel? Is my posture good? Do I remember to tighten my abdominals? Are my feet aligned properly? Is my breathing controlled?" I really practice saying these things to myself when I am working out because my mind has a tendency to wonder when I'm listening to music, watching someone exercising incorrectly, or admiring what I call "a whole lot of man." This helps me refocus and bring my body back into balance with my workout. It really works.

- **Wear Something That Stimulates You-** My mood often determines the color of my clothes. I see so many people who wear all black while exercising, and many of them (not all) look like they are barely getting through their workout. When I wear my cute red Super Girl underwear, I feel super energized just knowing I have them on. Try wearing red for its high energy and passionate effect. Purple will help you focus and feel empowered to complete the task. Wearing yellow helps me to be creative and think of new and exciting projects to work on. I like wearing blue when taking yoga or palettes; it helps me to relax and become more flexible. I can't leave out PINK, I feel like a survivor and a WARRIOR.

- **Turn Your Mind into A Virtual Experience-** It's easy and its fun. Now that you are more in tune with how your body is responding during your workout, visualize how you are going to look when you attend that special event or take that wonderful vacation. Here are some of the things I tell myself when I really get my work out on.

  o "My arms are going to be nice and toned for that red dress I just bought"

- o "My abs will be nice and tight in my swimsuit this summer."
- o "My cute little legs are going to look so shapely in my pumps."
- o "This is going to keep my back muscles good and strong and help relieve
- o that nagging back pain I sometimes get."
- o "When I finished working out, I'm going to be in such a good mood."

As you build your workout, you will create your own personal affirmations that will help take your motivation and commitment to a whole new level. Try it on for size; it just may be a good fit. I would love to hear what they are, so please share them with me on my website by email.

SECTION SEVEN

Should I Even Wear a Bathing Suit?

Since this is what started it all, let's talk about proper swimwear styles for your particular body shape. First things first, determine your body shape and measurements. Yes, the true size of your bust, hips, and waist. Do this in the privacy of your home when nobody's watching. With a measuring tape, wrap it around your back crossing the full part of the breast. Do the same for the waste but be sure to measure right above your navel. Now for the good stuff, measure the hips at the fullest part around your rump. Lastly, measure the torso by starting from the shoulder to mid-breast and from there to the crotch. Make sure to write these down and take them with you when you go shopping.

I like wearing a certain style of bathing suit because of my banana shape and skinny legs. If you are straight up and down like me, the sporty type suits with swooping necklines, hip-hugger bottoms, and racer back tops are for you. Tankinis and the traditional one-piece suits flatter my figure best while bikinis and French cut suits make me look anorexic. Adding volume is always a good idea only if you're into bows and ruffles. Any bathing suit won't do; it has to fit properly; otherwise, it may be hard on the eyes. Remember when it comes to your body shape, "It is what it is," and that doesn't have to be the perfect hourglass figure.

But if you are blessed enough to have the perfect hourglass curves, don't hesitate to show them off. Go with the boldest colors you can find in a one-piece or bikini that shows off your headlights and hips while pulling attention away from your waist. I love the plunging necklines, crisscross straps, and halter tops on this shape, and adding a little bling can really accent your curves up and down. If you are the appetizing apple of someone's eye, then your goal should be to pump up the derriere. Less is better. Go with a slightly smaller bottom to look more proportionate. A lighter top and dark bottom gives a great illusion of balance. Have fun with this; it can really be an attention grabber.

Pear shape ladies don't feel left out. Darker color bathing suits, especially one-piece, can make you look thinner in the hips. The tankini seems to work well if you are heavy on the bottom. Don't worry; these can have a pattern, but a small, cute one. If you have rather large knockers and don't want to show them off, just make sure it fits and provides adequate support. It's always nice to leave something to the imagination.

For any of these shapes, focus on drawing attention towards the breast area. Don't be afraid to add some support upstairs. Silicone inserts work wonders, and they stay in place while swimming. Be careful when it comes to wearing the skirt or boy short cut, you might look more bottom-heavy than you are. And belts? Well, does anybody wear bathing suits with belts anymore? Unless you're Twiggy (youngsters you may have to Google her) stay away from them, they simply attract too much attention. Whichever, you choose, remember you'll look a whole lot better if you're in good shape.

SECTION EIGHT

Standing Ovations

What is the part or parts of your body you like the most? This is always one of my first questions for my clients. I need to determine rather or not they feel they have any, and secondly, what they are. I realized that there is usually at least one physical characteristic a person likes or maybe even loves about themselves; this could be a specific body part, shape, or height. For me, it's my arms and my thighs. Even with my skinny calves and ankles, my quadriceps always look great, and I get compliments all the time. I would focus more of my workouts on areas that I want extra definition and tone, like my calves, gluteus (butt), and abdominals. Once you decide to commit to an exercise routine, remember that the smallest steps in the right direction is a huge success. Below are testimonies of real women who committed themselves to the challenge of improving their outlook on exercise and getting in shape. Please feel free to share your standing ovation with me.

What If I Finally Find Mr. Right?

Carmen

Age: 38

Body Shape: Pear

Motivation: Honeymoon

Best Asset: Legs

Focus: Upper Body

Exercise Level: Beginner

Goal: Tone

Carmen really disliked her size and shape, and more than that, she hated the thought of going to the gym. Working out was like a second job, and after getting off work, she just wanted to go home and chill. Even though she was 80lbs overweight, she couldn't motivate herself enough, to even go for a walk. After many years of living a single life, she finally met her best friend and husband-to-be. Now she hated how she allowed herself to get so heavy and out of shape. And now, with a new fiancée that loves to travel, she dreads putting on a bathing suit or wearing a sundress. Even though she has nicely shaped legs, they were not firm. She was used to hiding her body beneath baggy clothes. This is unfortunate because Carmen is an attractive lady with a beautiful face.

When Carmen came to me, she was in tears, and it didn't matter how much her fiancé said he loves just the way she is. She didn't like herself and was finally ready to do something about it. I designed a very basic workout plan for her that consisted mostly of cardio activities and some very light weights. Of course, this is only half the battle; a total fitness program consists of healthy nutrition and regular exercise. But this was a good start. Along with personal training sessions three days per week, Carmen fell in love with Zumba, the workout that combines Latin and other music to burn stubborn calories. She loves to dance and shake her booty. Carmen wanted to have more tone and definition in her arms, chest, and abdominal muscles. After 10 weeks of working out together, she was on her way. Six months later and before her first cruise to the Caribbean, Carmen lost a whole 24 lbs., an average of 4 pounds a month. Not bad for someone that hated working out.

Carmen's Workout

Target Area	Exercise	LBS	SETS	REPS	Work That Body Plan
Arms	Seated Biceps curl Machine Triceps Extension	5	3	10-15	• Zumba • 1-2 exercises per target area • 2-3 times per week • Light hand and machine weights • Training Session: 10 Weeks
Chest	Chest press	10	2	15	**Note:**
Back	Seated Vertical Row	20	2	10	✓ To tone muscles, use less weight with higher repetitions
Abdominals	Abdominal Crunches	—	2	15	✓ To build muscles use more weight with lower repetitions
Legs	Leg Extension Hamstring Curl	20	2	10	

Zumba Tip: Work at your own pace and choose someone in the class to follow to learn the moves, and they won't even know. A regular member in my Zumba class is a lady in a motorized wheelchair, she moves her arms and legs to the sound of the upbeat music, and she gets a great workout. So, try it out and just have fun.

Did You Know??? Regular exercise can reduce the risk of heart disease and diabetes.

What If I Get Divorced?

Lisa

Age: 52

Body Shape: Apple

Motivation: Dating

Best Asset: Buttocks

Focus: Total Body

Exercise Level: Beginner

Goal: Lose Weight, Tone

After twenty years of marital bliss, Lisa's husband decided he didn't want to be married anymore, at least to Lisa. He decided to leave home, file for divorce, leaving Lisa devastated. For whatever reason, men seem to move on so much easier and faster than women, big bellies, flabby bodies, and all. Besides the thought of having to adjust to living alone for the first time in twenty years, she was totally out of shape. She wanted to start dating again right away. Lisa was a big lady, and with so many years of a sedentary lifestyle, she was in for a rude awakening.

When Lisa came to me, she wanted instant results. She wanted to lose twenty pounds right away, and there was no talking her out of it. She insisted that I work her out long and hard. I explained that this was not the best approach and why, and she needed to build up her strength and endurance first and foremost. I agreed to design a workout for her that I thought, with commitment and modifying her dietary intake could help her reach her goal. She admitted that giving up her love late-night snacking and lots of cold beer was going to be difficult, but she was willing to give it a try. Lisa only agreed to 8 sessions with and they were well worth it. This gave me the opportunity to share with her the many health benefits of an active lifestyle and the importance of good nutrition. She soon started to realize that exercise and losing weight took commitment and patience. And as God is my witness, when I ran into Lisa at the grocery store some four months later, I hardly recognized her. She had lost 15 lbs. and was looking healthier and a lot happier. I didn't get a chance to ask her how the dating game was going.

Lisa's Workout

Target Area	Exercise	LBS	SETS	REPS	Work That Body Plan
Arms	Standing Biceps curl Triceps Push Down	3-5	3	10-15	• Treadmill (30-45 minutes) • 1-2 exercises per target area • Two times per week • Light hand and machine weights • Training Session: 4
Chest	Knee Push-Ups	—	2	10	
Back	Machine Back Extension	—	2	10	**Note:** ✓ A moderately intense treadmill
Abdominals	Abdominal Machine	20	2	10	session of 30 minutes or more can
Legs	Squats	—	3	10	significantly improve your health

Treadmill Tip:

Avoid growing bored with your treadmill routine by incorporating interval training. For example, after warming up, increase your speed for the next 1-2 minutes and then return to average speed for the next 4-5 minutes. Then repeat for a burst of fat burning.

Did You Know??? Aerobic exercise assists in revving up metabolism, making it easier to lower the percentage of body fat.

What If I Want to Have a Baby?

Marietta

Age: 27

Body Shape: Hourglass

Motivation: Pregnancy

Best Asset: Chest and Thighs

Focus: Core

Exercise Level: Beginner

Marietta and her husband had been trying to have a baby for several years. The first two pregnancies ended in miscarriage, but she was not going to give up. Even though she worked out occasionally, she was concerned that too much exercise would lower her chances of getting pregnant. When I explained that working out and building strong muscles would greatly enhance her ability to deliver the baby and help her recover faster, she started to see things differently. She had no prescribed orders from her personal physician not to exercise.

Exercise during pregnancy promotes better rest and decrease the risk of complications. I found that many understood the concept of pregnancy and childbirth, but not the total physiology of it. For example, the fetus (baby) is not really in the stomach, get the picture?

Marietta's Workout

Target Area	Exercise	LBS	SETS	REPS	Work That Body Plan
Arms	Biceps curl Triceps Extension	5-10	3	10	• Elliptical Machine (30-45 mins) • 1-2 exercises per target area • Three times per week
Chest	Dumbbells Fly	—	2	10	• Hand and machine weights • Training Session: 12 Weeks
Back	Lap Pull Down	—	2	10	Note:
Abdominals	Bicycle Leg Raises Exercise Ball Crunch	—	2	15	✓ The Elliptical Machine is a great workout for the whole body without impacting the joints.
Legs	Lunges	—	3	10	

Elliptical Tip: Backward motion on the elliptical machine is a great workout for the gluteus (butt) muscles

Did You Know???

The initial weight loss from exercise will be from areas of the body that store the most fat, for example, the thighs and the hips. So, hang in there to start melting belly fat.

What if I'm Invited to A Formal Affair?

Bonnie

Age: 45

Body Shape: Banana

Motivation: Formal Event

Best Asset: Shoulders

Focus: Shoulders and Back

Exercise Level: Intermediate

Bonnie was a regular member of the women's gym, where I worked. She loved walking the outside track and taking a variety of aerobics classes. She never particularly cared for weight training because she was under the false impression that she would bulk up like a man. During the previous year, Bonnie dropped 10 lbs., and was quite comfortable with her weight. That was until she was invited to a formal event coming up in three months. After trying on several dresses and noticing bulges in places that she never paid attention to, particularly her back, she decided to try some personal training sessions.

When Bonnie came to me, I explained how aerobic exercises are great for the cardiovascular system and building endurance but do little for toning and strengthening muscles. I also dispelled that myth about bulking up by helping her to understand the role of female (Estrogen) and male (Testosterone) hormones and how they function. Excited and enlightened by this information, she began to add weights to her workout routine.

Bonnie's Workout

Target Area	Exercise	LBS	SETS	REPS	Work That Body Plan
Arms	Shoulder Press Lateral Raises Butterfly	5-10	3	10	• Class: Stretch and Tone • Cardio: Spinning/Cycle • 2-3 exercises per target area • Three times per week • Hand and machine weights • Training Session: 12 Weeks
Chest	Dumbbells Fly	5-10	3	10	
Back	One –Arm Row	5-10	3	10	Note:
Abdominals	Reverse Crunch	—	2	10	✓ Cycling allows you to pedal at your own pace while feeling the energy and team spit of those around you.
Legs	Leg Press	30-40	3	10	

Spinning Tip: Try mentally visualizing your favorite locations, like the Golden Gate Bridge or the beach, and if the music is boring, no one will frown if you're taking off to the sounds of your own beats. Just be sure to wear your earplugs.

Did You Know???

Transitional fat (also known as Trans Fat) is very harmful and increases bad cholesterol as well as transfer fatty deposits to other vital parts of the body.

How Can I Prevent Losing My Mind?

Jan was a 62-year-old corporate executive looking forward to retiring in three years. The years of working in a high-paced environment for so many years left Jan feeling stressed and anxious. Throughout Jan's life, she frequently thought about working out but didn't have the time or the energy to do so. Jan went to her doctor for a check-up and was prescribed adequate rest and exercise. Staying physically active helps to produce endorphins and other chemicals in the brain that reduces stress, relieves irritability, improves sleep, and increases energy. She started on five different cardio exercises, which included walking, cycling, stair claiming, aqua aerobics, and Zumba Gold. We worked out together side-by-side three times per week for 30-45 minutes, and after six months, Jan was feeling good and optimistic about life and retirement.

What Will They Think of Me During the Interview?

Linda has always been self-conscious about her extra weight; unsuccessful fad diets had only been discouraging over the years. Linda did not realize that these diets only assisted weight loss and could not miraculously melt the pounds away. After her job downsized, 49-year-old Linda was thrown back into the job market after almost ten years. Now she was older and heavier than she had ever been and frightened to death that she would be judged based on her size and not her knowledge, skills, and abilities to perform the job. Studies have shown that discrimination does exist against obese job candidates more so than what a person wears or how badly they do in the interview. Linda's goal was simply to drop a few dress sizes so that she would look good in her clothes while boosting her confidence for future job opportunities. I recommended that Linda continue with her current nutritional modification routine while adding a combination of aerobic and strength training to decrease fat mass and build lean muscles. Our workout consisted of weights and cardio circuit routines, which kept Linda moving quickly between exercises (barbells, strength machines, elliptical, etc.) in an effort to burn more calories than the slower-paced workouts. Linda fell in love with the circuit station and ultimately loss two dress sizes, about 10 pounds. Eventually, she ended up finding another job.

Besides a Pedicure, What Else Could I Do to My Toes?

Sarah was an active 68 years young, who took 3-4 aerobics classes a week. She had previously undergone a total hip and knee replacement. Sarah's one desire was to stay active and mobile, especially since the surgeries. The one area that Sarah never focused on, although she knew this was important, was incorporating a good stretching routine into her workout. Stretching is equally important as working out, and in Sarah's case, it is especially important. When it comes to this part of the workout routine, the pros definitely outweigh the cons by improving range of motion, flexibility, energy, circulation, and prevention of injury. It only took three sessions for Sarah to learn how to properly stretch her biceps, triceps, hamstring, quadriceps, and calf, and back muscles. The next time we ran into each other, she was excited to demonstrate how she could now touch her toes.

Cassey (21) wanted to "Flaunt A Six-Pack Instead of Drinking One" after breaking up with her beer-guzzling boyfriend. She was quite physically active at school already but wanted to work exclusively on her abdominals. (See my Abdominal Specialization Routine.)

Cynthia (37) loves to "Strut the Latest Styles." As a "shoe fashionista," Cynthia's main goal in life was to always be on top of the designer's latest fashions and looking good in them was a must. She wanted to work out her legs. (See my Leg Specialization Routine).

Ann (72) wanted to work out to get strong for her pending abdominal surgery and recovery. We worked on core building exercises.

Kathy (56) wanted to improve her sex life by increasing her stamina and endurance. Cardio, cardio, cardio was the name of the game.

Ella (42) wanted to enter a beauty contest for mommies. This required a total body workout routine.

Jessica (24) wanted to be strong enough to defend herself and fight off an attacker. My martial arts training helped me to develop a kicking, striking, and punching routine for her that would give any attacker a second thought.

Karen (31) wanted to feel confident while prancing around in the nude; she was a stripper and exotic dancer. Total body workout.

Phyllis (57) just wanted to "Get A Good Night's Sleep" after being slapped with a relentless bout of insomnia. Her doctor recommended exercise instead of pills. We took this workout outside for some modified boot camp and circuit training. (See my Park Circuit Routine).

These standing ovations reflect the motivation and dedication it took to either ramp up their workout routines, jump back into exercising after a hiatus, or start out for the very first time. In any case, all were encouraged to work with their own unique size, shape, physical attributes, and fitness levels, allowing them to enjoy working out and the many health benefits that comes with it.

Conclusion

Each one of us is created uniquely based on our culture and genetics. We represent a rainbow of sizes, shapes, and colors. The human landscape is one in which we can build upon or tear down during this lifetime. The quality of our lives is heavily influenced by how much we value our ourselves. It's never too late to modify our lifestyles to reflect this. Although modern medicine offer so many ways to alter our outer appearance and enhance our self-image, we are still the master of our destiny when it comes to maintaining our health. What if many of the people I was observing that day by the pool would have thought years earlier, "I don't want to be fat and out of shape when I get older," or "I want to be healthy and feel good about myself as I grow older," and actually did something about it? I think they would be living happier, healthier, and longer lives today.

I truly believe my entire life would have been different had I not developed a passion for exercise. It helps me to be physically, emotionally, and spiritually strong. Exercising gave me the strength to rebound from a major (7-hour) breast reconstructive surgery in record time. I went home the same day because the doctor had that much confidence in my ability to recover at home with no complications. I go to the gym or workout rain or shine and sometimes when it's the last thing on earth I want to. I exercised with others, and on my own, and I feel great afterwards. So can you.

Please remember that you are all you have, so cherish this vessel called the human body as much as possible. If you haven't already, start a wonderful journey of health and wellness, and I promise you, you will never regret it. If a blind man is inspired to walk his dog every day, a woman with cerebral palsy can climb onto exercise equipment, or a bilateral amputee can lift weights, there's no excuse. Your shape is your shape and your size is your size, work with what you got. Some days, weeks, and months will be better than others, so what, regroup and get back into it. You'll be so glad you did. It has truly been my desire to inspire and motivate you to embrace a healthy and rewarding lifestyle, so get up and…. WORK THAT BODY NOW!

Abdominal Specialization Routine

Photo by Jonathan Borba

Complete three sets of 10 reps. Mix and Match until you achieve 30 reps per workout.

Remember to breath.

- **Abdominal Crunches**
  - o Lie down on your back and bend both knees with hands behind your head (do not bend the neck) or cross your chest, slowly raise your shoulder blades off the floor, approximately 1-3 inches, return, and repeat.

- **Stability Ball Crunches**
  - o Sit on the ball and walk your feet forward until your body is parallel to the floor, place your hand behind your neck for support and lift your upper body at a 45-degree angle. Relax and move slowly, return, and repeat.

- **Reverse Crunch (flat or on a slanted bench)**
  - o Lay on your back with arms stretch and palms down on each side of your body than with your feet together, pull up the knees towards the chest, return, and repeat.

- **Bicycle Crunches**
  - o Lying on your back with hands on the side of your head, raise one leg off the floor and extend, raise the other leg

and bend knee towards the chest, twist through your core for a good workout, repeat.

- **Cross Leg Crunches**
  - o Start in a crunch position and place the right ankle on the left bent knee, then begin crunch exercise, repeat on the opposite knee.

- **Oblique Crunches**
  - o Assume the position for the abdominal crunch but now twist to the right or left side and lift. Complete one side at a time or alternate.

- **Weighted Sit-Ups (Use 5-10lb weight across the chest)**
  - o Lay flat on your back with the knees bent. If you are not able to lift up without raising your feet, someone can assist by holding the legs or feet. The feet can be anchored under a sofa or the bed frame. Hold a 5-10lb barbell across the chest and sit-up as far as you can. Perform this exercise at the gym easily also.

- **Hanging Knee Raises**
  - o This exercise really isolates the abdominal muscles for a great workout. Hang from a pull-up bar or leg lift machine and slowly raise your knees up to the chest. Hold for a moment and repeat. This is a controlled exercise. Take your time.

- **Deadbug**
  - o Lie on your back with knees bent, hold the arms straight up, now extend the right arm and the left leg, keep the back flat and squeeze the abdominal muscles, alternate with the opposite leg and arm.

- **Plank**

  o Bend your knees and sit on your heels, walk the hands out and extend the legs and align the shoulders and lower body to form a straight line, hold for 30 to 60 seconds, repeat.

- **Wide Toe Touches**

  o Lie on your back and bring both legs up to form an L position. Now stretch and touch your toes, repeat.

Leg Specialization Routine

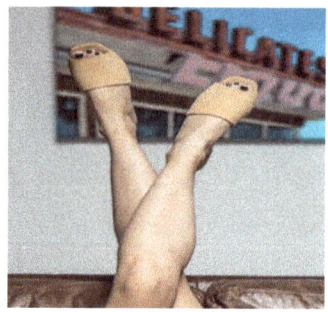

Photo by Oz Seyrek

Complete all exercises for a total workout three times per week.

- **Squats with 5-10 lbs. weight- 3 sets of 8**

  o Keep your head up, torso straight, and abdominals tight during the squat, keep the knees behind your toes, and the hips down and back. This is an excellent toning exercise.

- **Leg Extension Machine – 3 sets of 10 (15-30 lbs.)**

  o Sit up straight with your back flat and abdominal muscles tight. This exercise isolates the quadriceps, making them firm and strong.

- **Thigh Curl Machine- 3 sets of 10 (15-30 lbs.)**

  o Sit on the machine with your lower legs over the padded bar then position the top bar over your thighs, next bend your legs without lifting your thighs. This is wonderful to work those often-forgotten hamstrings.

- **Lunges- -3 sets of 15 (5-10 lbs. barbell, Optional)**
  - o Hold a barbell in each hand and alternate a single-leg lung. Now you're working the quadriceps, gluteus muscles (butt), and hamstrings. Now that's a workout.

- **Outer Thigh Machine- 3 sets of 15 (15-25 lbs.)**
  - o Sit on the outer thigh machine and spread your thighs (abduction).
  - o This exercise targets the outer hip muscles, the large and small muscles of the gluteus (butt).

- **Inner Thigh Machine- 3 sets of 15 (15-25 lbs.)**
  - o Sit on inner thigh machine and squeeze (adduction) with both thighs, brace the abdominal muscles, and keep your back straight. This strengthens the inner thigh muscles.

- **Standing Toe Raises- 3 sets of 10 (10-15bs.)**
  - o This can be performed with the standing machine, with or without barbells
  - o (10-15 lbs.) Standing straight with the weight on your shoulders or by your side, raise the toes as high as you can up and down to build the calf muscles.

- **Seated Toe Raises- 3sets of 10 (20-30 lbs.)**
  - o These can be performed at the gym or at home using a chair with or without ankle weights. While seated, keep the back straight and raise or point the toes to get a great calf workout.

Park Circuit Workout

Perform this easy and effective "Do-It-Yourself" circuit exercises at any park or recreational area that offers a fitness trail and/or exercise stations. The park I frequent has a 1.1-mile trail with ten workout stations that circle a beautiful lake. There are also several small baseball bleachers and park benches which are great for stair-stepping and other exercises.

1. Stretch (5-10 mins)

    - Biceps/Triceps Stretch

    - Quadriceps (Thighs)

    - Calf/Hamstring Stretch

    - Back

2. Warm-Up (10 Reps each)

    - Arm circles (front/back)

    - Side twist

    - Alternate Toe tap (Spread legs and alternate tapping out each foot)

3. Run or walk briskly to each station and perform the following exercises. If your park doesn't have stations then identify landmarks such as light poles, park benches, trees, etc.

    Exercise 1- Alternating Lunges (10 Reps Each Leg)

    Exercise 2- Jumping/Walking Jacks (25)

    Exercise 3- Stair Stepping (Bleachers 15-20)

    Exercise 4- Squats (Bike Rake) 10

    Exercise 5- Slanting Leg Stretch (10 seconds)

    Exercise 6- Bench Push-Up (10)

    Exercise 7- Bench Crunches (10)

    Exercise 8- Bench Triceps Push Downs (8-10)

    Exercise 9- Alternating Windmill Leg Exercises

    Exercise 10- Reverse Leg Lift (10 Reps Each Leg) Park Bench/ Bike Rack

Repeat 1-3 times, depending on your endurance and physical ability. These exercises can be modified for your workout level by performing some and not others, decreasing or increasing the repetitions. Exhale on the exertion part of the exercise. Stop and stretch in between; it feels great. Make it your own.

Photos by Pamela
Marshall

 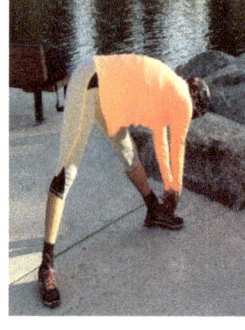 

Back Stretch   Inner Leg Stretch   Calf Stretch

Quadricep Stretch 1   Quadricep Stretch 2   Squat

Walking Lunge   Alternating Windmills   Arm Stretch

Inner Thigh Stretch   Tricep Stretch   Upper Body Stretch

Resistance Band and Barbell Exercises

Bicep Curl | Triceps Extension Begin | Triceps Extension Front View

Tricep Extension Back View | Barbell Bicep Curl Beg | Barbell Bicep Curl Finish

Barbell Tricep Extension

94

Work That Body Journal

Date: _____

Target Area	Exercise	LBS	SETS	REPS	Cardio
LEGS					
BACK					
CHEST					
SHOULDERS					
ARMS (Biceps/Triceps)					
ABDOMINALS					

References

http://www.shopyourshape.com, Jan 28, 2014

http://www.Today.com/style/body/hair-flab-more-store-mannequins-get -makeovers, Jan 28, 2014

http://en.wikipedia.org/wiki/Louisiana_Creole_people

http://repository.lib.ncsu.edu/ir/bitstream/1840.16/1820/1/etd.pdf

http://www.hindawi.com/journals/jobe/2013/542736/

http://www.ncbi.nlm.nih.gov/pubmed/20981637

http://ohioline.osu.edu/hyg-fact/5000/pdf/5255.pdf

http://www.nationaldairycouncil.org/SiteCollectionDocuments/education_materials/hispanic_heath_kit
/LAHIDAN_HealthImplications_FinalProof.pdf

http://www.sciencedaily.com/releases/2013/12/131219131039.htm

http://www.medicaldaily.com/losing-weight-harder-black-women-same-diet-white-women-265599

http://clinical.diabetesjournals.org/content/22/4/190.full

http://en.wikipedia.org/wiki/Female_body_shape

http://healthpsych.psy.vanderbilt.edu/2009/AfricanAmericanBodyImage.htm

http://www.calculator.net/body-type-calculator.html

http://www.explore-hispanic-culture.com/hispanic-culture.html

http://fashion.about.com/cs/tipsadvice/a/allaboutfit_3.htm

http://deepblue.lib.umich.edu/bitstream/handle/2027.42/97941/meiguan_1.pdf?sequence=1

http://www.topix.com/forum/afam/TDVLN2IMP9EL4KLUP

http://www.sheknows.com/beauty-and-style/articles/

www.ingramcontent.com/pod-product-compliance
Lightning Source LLC
Chambersburg PA
CBHW051224120626
46547CB00013B/1493